Lilah's Gift

by Lynn Cullen

illustrated by Mary Collier

MODERN CURRICULUM PRESS

Pearson Learning Group

Lilah held the puppy next to her cheek. The pup made squeaking sounds and began licking.

"You can't keep it," said Lilah's older sister, Rebecca.

"Not it," said Lilah as the pup kept licking. "Lolly. His name is Lolly, short for lollipop."

The puppy thought the world was his lollipop.

"Just because it's the only one left, doesn't mean it can stay," said Rebecca.

Lilah said nothing. She wondered how soon it would be before Lolly could jump up on her bed. Lolly's mother, Daisy, always slept on Rebecca's bed.

Rebecca got to select Daisy from the shelter three years ago. Even though she had short legs, Daisy was good at jumping up on furniture. Lolly would be too.

"We can only keep one dog," said Rebecca, "and that's Daisy."

Lilah held up her chin to let the pup lick it. Lolly was smart. He had known Lilah's scent even before his eyes opened. Whenever Lilah got near the pups, he came to her. He knew who loved him best.

"Go ahead and ignore me. It doesn't change anything," said Rebecca.

The next day in school, Lilah stared out the window. Mrs. Goodman was explaining their science lesson. She asked a boy to select a picture of a reptile.

Lilah didn't hear her. She was trying to figure out how to keep Lolly. She was convinced that there was a way. How could a person love a pup as much as she loved Lolly and let him go?

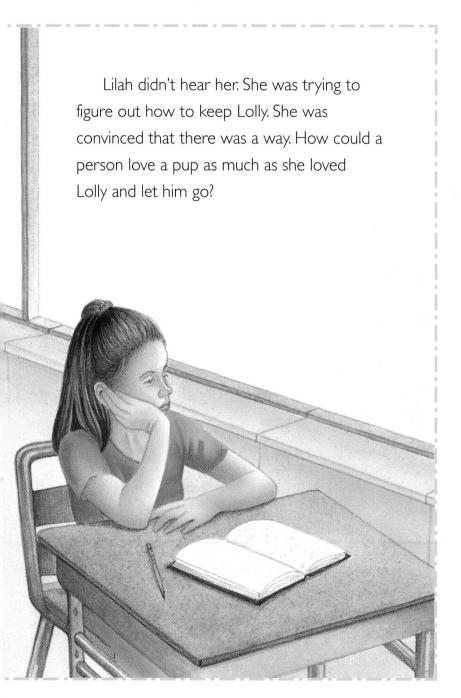

Outside, a woman wheeled a stroller into
the schoolyard. Lilah's heart knotted when
she saw the short-legged, long-haired dog at
the woman's feet.

Lolly might look like that someday.

The woman unstrapped a toddler from the stroller. The minute she was free, the little girl ran for the slide. Her red dress blew in the wind. The mother selected a bench and sat down. She opened a book. The dog sat at the woman's feet.

Maybe someday Lolly would sit in a park at Lilah's feet.

Something red fluttering near the slide caught Lilah's eye. Horrified, she saw the girl fall off the slide to the wood chips below.

Lilah panicked. "The girl fell!" she yelled, popping out of her chair.

Mrs. Goodman frowned. "What?"

"Outside!" yelled Lilah.

They all jumped out of their seats.

To Lilah's amazement, the mother kept reading while the girl lay on the ground crying. The dog sprang to his feet. He barked at the woman. Then he darted to the girl.

The woman screamed. Then she bolted to her child and swept her up. The dog stood nearby, rigid and alert.

At last the mother put the child down. The
little girl trotted back to the slide. This time
she held her mother's hand. The class sighed
with relief.

"Why did that lady keep on reading when her
little girl was crying?" Lilah asked. "She should have
run to the girl immediately."

Mrs. Goodman gazed out the window.
"I don't think the woman can hear, Lilah.
I believe her dog listened for her and then
alerted her. I've heard of dogs for the hearing
impaired. Now I think I've finally seen one."
She had a look of awe on her face.

The class resumed their lesson. But Lilah
still wasn't listening. She was beginning to
get an idea.

When Lilah got home, a sign sat on the kitchen table.

FREE PUP TO GOOD HOME

Lilah's mother turned from the sink. "I'm sorry, Lilah. We can't possibly keep another dog. This house is already too crowded for the five of us." She hugged Lilah.

"Don't look so horrified, baby. Letting him go seems hard now. But you'll feel better in time."

"I think I know a way to feel better now." Lilah drew in a breath. "Can my pup be a hearing ear dog?"

Before Lilah could regret it, she had her mother call the Humane Shelter. Mrs. Goodman had said they knew a great deal about hearing ear dogs there.

"Someone will come over tomorrow," said Lilah's mother. "They like to select puppies just the age of Daisy's pup. They want dogs that will grow up to be small to mid-sized."

"Like Lolly," said Lilah. She felt panicked for just a moment. Lolly was really leaving.

"If Lolly would be a good dog for training, the Humane Shelter will help get him into a program. The dogs have to understand if there is danger," said Lilah's mother. "The trainers only select the smartest pups."

"That's Lolly," Lilah said.

"The dogs have be able to jump up on beds. One of their jobs is to lick their masters awake."

Lilah closed her eyes. *Lolly*.

Lilah's mother gathered Lilah into her arms. "What a great idea. You're doing a wonderful thing. I'm in awe of you."

Lilah swallowed back the lump in her throat. It was Lolly who deserved her mother's awe. Lilah just knew what she had known from the start. Lolly was the best dog ever.